The Peaceful Soul

Reflective Steps Toward Awareness

Margot Robinson

I am convinced that many generations will benefit from Margot Robinson's clear thinking and truly profound inspiration. There is nothing that I have seen, read, or experienced, that guides people as well as this book on how to take control and responsibility for their own lives and happiness. This is a must read!

Carol Anderson Taber
Publisher Working Mother Magazine

Revised Printing

KENDALL/HUNT PUBLISHING COMPANY
4050 Westmark Drive Dubuque, Iowa 52002

This book is dedicated
to my loving

Revised Printing

Library of Congress Catalog Card Number: 97-70033

ISBN 0-7872-3532-6

Printed in the United States of America
10 9 8 7 6 5 4 3 2

TABLE OF CONTENTS

The drawings shown throughout **The Peaceful Soul Within** are mine. Creating them has helped me during difficult times in my life. They have found a home within this book.

ACKNOWLEDGMENTS

No book can be written without having others involved. It has been such a pleasure to work with each of these people. They have given me strength and a wealth of ideas.

My idea crew:

Alice Barsony
Jane Martin
April Hutchinson
Dr. Jim Harris
Joel Blackwell
Betsy Robinson Smith
Heather Robinson Reimann
Betty McGurk
Patsy Kendall
Dr. Thomas Benson
Dr. Pat Bailey
Dick Wolfe
Courtenay Huff
Dr. Joe Palladino
Brenda McClain
Janet Fox
Barbara Mintzer-McMahon
Karen Mundy
Kira Robinson
Sherry Poole-Clark

And last to my husband Stephen Planson –Without his encouragement, I would not be the person I am today. I am thankful to be able to experience my life with him.

NOTE FROM AUTHOR

I was in emotional pain for many years of my life, pain that choked off my lifeline. I was an unhappy person desperate for peace, spending years working hard to obtain the inner peace I found so elusive. This peace, I thought, would send a lifeboat to my dying self-esteem, would bring me inner harmony, and let me look in the mirror and be glad that it was me staring back.

My message is that once you can find your avenue and then learn to thrive, life will blossom and you will have peace within.

So many people I see in my work, on TV, or whom I read about in newspapers are as unhappy as I was. It is for those people I wrote this book.

One day I watched a spider walk across a box — it took all of four seconds. The spider moved so naturally, seemingly without effort.

My life has not been this effortless. I experienced pain, roadblocks, and despair until I learned how to take charge of my life and learned how to have peace within.

INTRODUCTION

It only took four seconds for the spider to walk across a box — it has taken me a lifetime to blossom.

"You may be whatever you resolve to be."

• Stonewall Jackson •

CHAPTER 1

My Story

"All the greatest and most important problems of life are fundamentally insolvable. They can never be solved, but only outgrown."

· Carl Jung ·

Thriving Message Number 1

Only you are responsible for your own thoughts and actions.

I am not sure when I was told that she had died. But ever since I can remember, I had known she was dead, and I had an empty feeling because she was gone. I didn't know where the emptiness came from.

I was depressed for so long and it took four decades for the feeling to leave. And it was not until I dealt with my mother's death that I became free. My mother died when I was two days old. My father hired a nurse to take care of me and my three siblings until I was ten months old when he married my stepmother, whom I refer to as my mom.

When I was eight years old, the next door neighbor told me that I was responsible for my mother's death. I interpreted this to mean that I murdered her. Of course, I said nothing, but I hated myself in silence. Then I began to overeat, hiding food under my bed. Within my family circle, I was called "Little Faye" for "fatty".

"A teacher who is attempting to teach without inspiring the pupil with a desire to learn is hammering on cold iron."

• Horace Mann •

The pain became a dark cloud that hung around me most of my life. It was when I went through that dark cloud and arrived at the other side that I began to thrive. The other side is like a garden. It is peaceful; it has no victims. It is a place where I can live only in the moment.

It is how life is meant to be.

DYSLEXIA

Besides losing my mother, I was born with a learning disability called dyslexia. Dyslexia comes from a Greek word, which means having difficulty with words and language. The best way to describe being dyslexic is that it is difficult to read, write, and spell. Expressing thoughts on paper is also very difficult. School was difficult because I was constantly told I wasn't smart. I was always put in the lowest reading group, the lowest spelling group, the lowest math group. It would be years before I was diagnosed as dyslexic.

Unfortunately, I didn't get positive reinforcements in school.

"There are three things which if a man does not know, he can not live long in the world: what is too much for him, what is too little for him, and what is just right for him."

• Zanzibar Proverb •

I wasn't encouraged where I did excel, such as art and my love for nature, because the teachers I had didn't know how to nourish wounded souls.

My fifth grade teacher made me stand in front of the class and read the word "discipline" from the dictionary. He thought I needed to be disciplined and if I read it out loud to the class, the class would agree. I couldn't read the words in front of me. I made something up, but it was not the definition. But he made me stand there and read every word for what seemed like hours. I could not pronounce the words, and everyone laughed. I was so humiliated that I wanted the earth to open and swallow me.

There were many days like that, and I began to hate everything about school.

OTHER PAIN

So much of my life was painful. Until I learned to thrive, it seemed like all the challenges I had on my path were too much to handle. I could not have children

> **"It is tragic how few people ever 'possess their souls' before they die."**
>
> **• Oscar Wilde •**

because of problems stemming from an IUD. I had many surgeries and physical illnesses such as diabetes. My first marriage was terrible. My husband was an alcoholic and was both physically and emotionally abusive to me. When I was single, I had a knack for picking the wrong man. For years my heart was constantly broken. I continued to place myself in the wrong job — even getting fired from one — until I changed within and found out who I was.

I responded as a powerless victim to most events. The forces outside of me had control, not me. I blamed everyone else, and I hated me.

MY HEALING JOURNEY BEGINS

I can remember the beginning of my healing journey as if it were yesterday. I found a job in fund-raising for a state school in North Carolina. With an extroverted personality, I thought I would be great at fund-raising. It turned out to be a secretarial job and I did not do well because of my learning disability.

After eleven months they let me go. The message was: "Margot, you're a flop again!"

But this time it was the end of the line. I would not sink to the bottom — this time I would fight back. After this event, I started to find out who I was.

There, from the bottom of the barrel, I started to pick myself up. I realized that I had played victim too many times. It was the only game I knew how to play, but now I wanted to move on.

" It matters not how straight the gate, how charged with punishment the scroll, I am the master of my fate; I am the captain of my soul."
· Henley ·

WHAT IS A VICTIM?

Victims have no power because they give their power to everyone else. They make no attempt to change — mostly because they're comfortable with that behavior. They know how to play the victim game and it's too hard to think about changing. It's too much work, so they make no attempt to grow and stretch.

As a victim, I blamed everything that came across my path.

"It's not my fault!"

"I'm not responsible!"

"I blame you for all
my problems."

Who did I blame? Mostly I blamed my problems on my mother who had left me. "Poor me", I thought and sought out people who would say, "that poor child".

BECOMING UNSTUCK

It was two days after I had been fired from my job with the State of North Carolina, that I realized I could no longer continue the destructive path I was following. I prayed a lot. I cried a lot. I sat in my chair in silence, just thinking.

Then it hit me. I was responsible for my thoughts and actions — I am in charge of my life. My birth mother certainly was not, but I had given her all the power — what a waste of energy! She was dead; she could do nothing. But I had the power to do everything.

With this realization, I began to stretch and grow. I decided to create the me I deserved to be. I wanted peace within.

My most recent "test" happened last summer. I was shocked to hear my doctor's words, "You have diabetes!" Within a month, I was giving myself shots just to stay alive. This time though, I had pulled all my skills together and made it from the black cloud to the garden very quickly. I chose not to be a victim, but to be responsible for me. To me, this experience was an obvious sign that I had learned how to thrive.

" I came, I saw, I conquered."

• Julius Caesar •

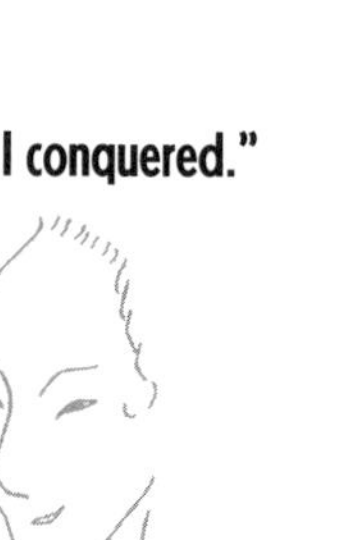

SO WHAT IS THRIVING?

Thriving means fighting to overcome your problems and difficulties. It is winning the battle and the war all at the same time. The war in my life was dealing with the loss of my mother at an early age. The battle was against depression, feeling empty, and my desire to give up on life.

I am truly alive today. I know I am responsible for me and no one else is. Thriving is about winning the war, winning the battle, and finding yourself.

THE VALUE OF THRIVING

When I look back on my life and see how mixed up I was, I say to myself, "I sure am thankful I am not a victim anymore." Thriving has brought calmness to my life. Where before there was turbulence, there is now peace.

Victims always have "stuff" hanging around their lives, prodding them to feel "Oh, poor me!". They are angry, hateful, depressed, sad, or just plain miserable. Just tune into any talk show. The air waves are full of victims. I don't think most people want to be victims, but they don't know any other way to act.

REFLECTIVE EXERCISES

Start a journal today and write your responses to the Reflective Exercises found at the end of each chapter.

- Reflect back on your life. Was there a time when you thought you were not responsible for your thoughts and actions?
- Did you blame others for your mistakes?
- Did you play the victim game? Write about these situations.
- Doing this will help you look at the big picture of your life as you learn to thrive.

CHAPTER 2

Stop the Fear

"Success is to be measured not so much by the position that one has reached in life as by the obstacle which he has overcome while trying to succeed."

• Booker T. Washington •

Thriving Message Number 2

We have to face our problems or they will continue to haunt us.

I joined the Army after college and it was there that I found out that I was dyslexic. An occupational therapist discovered my dyslexia, and I remember it was as if a huge weight was lifted off my shoulders. "You mean I am not stupid?", I asked.

Throughout my life I had to create systems (for math, reading, cooking, and visualizing outcomes of projects) that were compatible with the way other people did things. I did not think much about these systems but when I found out most people didn't create them, I was surprised. I thought everyone did.

A year and a half after I found out I was dyslexic, I enrolled in graduate school. I got higher grades there than I did throughout the rest of my education. Why? Because I was beginning to believe in myself and I was taking classes I really enjoyed. But I was still ashamed

"You gain strength, courage and confidence by every experience in which you really stop to look fear in the face. You are able to say to yourself, "I lived through this horror. I can take the next thing that comes along." You must do the thing you think you can not do."

• Eleanor Roosevelt •

of my dyslexia. For the next twelve years I acknowledged this problem to myself, but I told no one and did nothing to overcome it. In short, I sat with my mouth closed and said nothing. I was determined not to bring it out of the closet.

For all those years I said nothing about my dyslexia to my employers. Finally, my dyslexia was getting in the way of a project I was working on, so I couldn't remain silent anymore. If I didn't say something about this problem, I would burst.

For weeks I practiced what to say to my employer. I lost sleep, felt anxious, and went over and over the conversation in my mind. "Why are you telling your boss? Do you really need to say something? You have been quiet for so long, why bother now?"

The day approached for the meeting, and I was tongue-tied. There was a huge lump in my throat. Oh boy, here goes....

"He who has conquered doubt and fear has conquered failure."
• James Allen •

After I had spit out my story, he asked, "Is this all you wanted to tell me? This isn't a big deal! My best friend from high school had a learning disability."

"What a relief to get this out," I thought. "But why did I keep this a secret so long? It really wasn't a big deal, was it?" Guess what? I started telling everyone. And their reaction also was, "Hey, that isn't such a big deal". So, I had faced my biggest fear, and it turned out not to be a big deal. I was proud that I finally let people know my "secret". It felt so good not to have the emotions pent up anymore. I was free from a huge burden, and I started to feel peace within – the type of peace I talked about in the first chapter, like being in a garden.

REFLECTIVE EXERCISE

- What fears do you have in your life? Make a list of them.
- How can you face them?
- How can you overcome them?
- How can you start bringing peace into your life?
- Is there something in your life that may not be such a "big deal?"

CHAPTER 3

See the Gifts

"There can be no rainbow without a cloud and a storm."

• J. H. Vincent •

Thriving Message Number 3

Embrace your problems, then look for the gifts.

When I was nine, my mom came in to say good night before she and my dad went out for the evening. When she leaned down to kiss me, she smelled so wonderful just as I imagined movie stars would smell. She sat on my bed for a few minutes and told me that when she was my age she wanted to be a movie star. What did I want to be?

Well, I had just finished my prayers and told God I wanted to be like everyone else. I really didn't want to be different anymore. Then she told me that we are all different and unique. We were put on this earth to do something. She said good night and walked out, closing the door behind her.

I began thinking, "What is different about me?" But all I could come up with were negative things. I was not smart and I did not excel at anything. So I said one more prayer before I went to sleep. "Dear God, let me be like everyone else." That felt best.

" **Every man is the architect of his own fortune.**"
• Sallust •

EMBRACE THE TRAGEDY

Once I feel the anger and the pain, I can embrace the tragedy. As crazy as this sounds, it's true. The faster you make peace with the tragedy, the sooner you will move on in your life.

When I got diabetes, I embraced it immediately. My doctor was amazed at how quickly I had accepted this chronic disease. He told me that rarely had he seen someone take total charge as fast.

But to me there was no other choice. I knew from past experiences that if I did not embrace diabetes, I would spend years in denial. From all that I have read and understood about diabetes, a large group of diabetics do not take care of themselves because they are still in denial. "Hey, I can't handle this!" they say.

The first step in embracing my diabetes was getting angry and mad. I felt the pain. I cried, screamed, and I got most of the pain out of my system. After experiencing the anger, I could finally start embracing the illness. Without experiencing this first step, I could not have done as well with my acceptance of the condition.

By embracing diabetes, I was able to look at the gifts I was given. I had to eat healthy foods all the time or I would become ill. I had to exercise on a regular schedule to keep my blood sugar levels down. I was reminded that I had to take care of myself because now I was precious cargo. While not really fragile, I needed to be aware of how I felt all the time so I could survive. To me these points are all gifts.

By embracing my dyslexia, I also realized that being different was good. There were gifts all around me, if only I opened up my eyes and looked.

The biggest gift from dyslexia was becoming aware of my creativity. I could see things differently. Getting out of "the box" and looking within for solutions helped me in my consulting practice. Now I was being hired because of my difference. Wow! That concept was a new one.

Embracing my shameful secret of dyslexia made me more sensitive to the people in my workshops. I could encourage people to let go of their extra baggage and stop being victims. If they wanted it to, life would flourish.

"The eternal stars shine out as soon as it is dark enough."

• Carlyle •

Remember: Every problem brings a gift. Sometimes the gift is small; other times there are many gifts. If you first embrace the problem, and then identify the gifts, life will blossom — life will become that garden of peace.

REFLECTIVE EXERCISE

- How are you unique?
- Why do you think you were put on this earth?
- What do you think your purpose is?
- Next, list your problems. Next to each problem, write down the steps you will take to embrace your problem. Then search for the gifts you receive from each problem.

CHAPTER 4

What You Resist, Persists

"All our limitations are in
our own minds."

• Orison Swett Marden •

Thriving Message Number 4

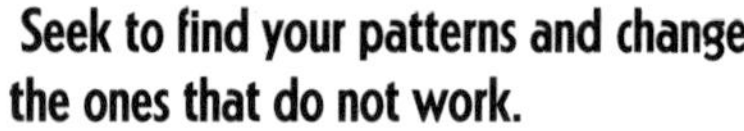

Seek to find your patterns and change the ones that do not work.

When I was about nine or ten, my mom noticed a pattern I had with my playmates. I would hold on to them and smother them. Some of my friends did not want to return to play with me because I was so possessive. She advised me to hold friendship with an open hand.

I smothered my friends because I was afraid that they were going to leave me as my birth mother had. It took years for me to realize this pattern: no one wants to be smothered and I was a smothering person.

So when it came to forming close relationships, I failed. Thus I had few friends, which added validity to my low self- esteem. "Since no one really likes me," I thought, "I must be bad." I continued that cycle of thinking for years.

Another pattern in my life involved my need to be perfect. If I was perfect, more people would love me. This need to be perfect was very strong, and I belittled myself if everything was not right. Then I would start the cycle all over again, never winning at the perfection game, but always trying — a lose-lose situation.

"Grief leads to comfort; suffering to patience."

• Singhalese Proverb •

As I reflect, another pattern I had was moodiness, which pushed people away from me. Who would want to be around someone so moody? No one. Moodiness was a great way to distance myself. Some of my moods were caused by a chemical imbalance, but most were caused by my unhappiness.

I was unhappy because I never was perfect. I wanted people to like me, but my behavior said, "Stay away from me." I had created a huge wall around myself. Outside, I was saying "Stay away," but inside I was crying, "Why doesn't anyone love me?"

To force people to like me, I would play the attention game. At school I was one of the class clowns. My trademark was tearing up paper and putting it down my dress, so that as I walked, paper would fall out. Everyone thought it was very funny. I would get the attention I craved for that moment, but it did not last long.

"**Our greatest glory is not in never falling, but in rising every time we fall."**
· Goldsmith ·

My self-esteem was so low that I could not say nice things about myself. I begged people to say I was doing great because I could not say that to myself. Little did I realize that few people wanted to pay attention to such an unhappy person. This self-sabotage would feed my low self-esteem and the cycle would continue. If anyone suggested ways that I could change and be happier, I saw it as criticism or rejection and I became hypersensitive — sometimes I even became hostile. Who would want to be around such a hostile, unhappy, attention-getting person?

When I was in high school, my twelfth-grade English teacher asked me what I wanted out of life. "All I want is to be happy," I told her. I was desperate for a sense of inner harmony.

When I finally started to deal with the loss of my mother, I found true freedom and inner harmony and started to thrive as an individual. But how did I deal with that loss?

It started when my favorite cat died. She was poisoned and died within hours. She was so young, and she and I had such a close bond. How could she have been taken from me at such an early age? The loss of my cat, along with having a hysterectomy a few months before, put me into an instant state of grief, and I mourned for a long time.

The next summer I went to Canada to visit my birth mother's brother. When I shared my pain with him, he said, "Your mother would not have wanted you to be like this. She was full of life and you should be too."

These words had a powerful influence on me. I began to deal with the loss of my cat — and the loss of my mother. I thought a lot;

" Sooner or later you act out what you really think."

• Japanese Proverb •

I talked to my current husband, and sought out counseling. In doing so, I chose not to be stuck anymore. I chose to go forward. I chose to be full of life.

REFLECTIVE EXERCISE

- List the patterns in your life. What patterns work?
- What patterns cause you problems?
- How can you live your life more fully?

CHAPTER 5

Use the Pain

"He who is not good to himself,
how can he be good to others?"

• Spanish Proverb •

Thriving Message Number 5

Feel the pain, acknowledge the pain, and then leave the pain behind by moving on with your life.

The first time my former husband hit me, I was in the Army working for Social Work Services. I was stunned by the abuse. I didn't understand why he had hit me — and so hard that my glasses flew across the room.

The morning after I was hit, I had to talk to someone. I could not tell anyone I worked with about what had happened the night before, so I went to the Chaplain's office. I told the woman behind the desk that I had to talk to someone right away. She could tell I was very upset. The Chaplain listened to me for 45 minutes, said a few things, and then shook his head. I was wondering if he understood my situation. To say the least, he was not very empathetic. During our talk, he had poor eye contact with me and at the end he said abruptly, "Our time is finished." He stood up, which was an indication that my time was up. I left very confused. What was I going to do? I never knew anyone who was physically

abused by her husband. What was my next step?

Then a basket of beautiful flowers was pushed into my hands. The receptionist said, "Your husband had these delivered here for you."

"Ask people's advice, but decide for yourself."

• Ukrainian Proverb •

I looked at the Chaplain. He smiled and said, "Now everything is going to be better," and walked away from me. How could he think everything would be better? I had a huge bruise on my left cheekbone, and it still hurt. What would I do if it happened again? What did these flowers have to do with the fact that my husband hit me?

I walked back into Social Work Services and asked a male friend if he was free for lunch. I had to talk about the abuse. Talking to him was like the difference between night and day. He listened, and he understood what emotional pain I was in. I did not feel I was crazy — as I had with the Chaplain. Because of my friend's understanding and caring attitude, I had found the right person to talk to during a very difficult time in my life.

"Whatever you can do, or dream you can, begin it. Boldness has genius, power and magic in it."

· Goethe ·

BEYOND SURVIVING

Once again, another haunting tragedy had come, and as always, it seemed unfair. "Poor me," I thought, "How am I going to handle this one?" Then consciously or subconsciously, I had to choose to be a victim or to empower myself.

Earlier in my life it was an easy choice for me — I was a victim every time, because I didn't know how to thrive. Even now, I am angry at first. I ask myself, "Why me? What did I do to deserve this?" The first thing I do is to feel the anger. And I really feel that emotion. That means I cry and am sad. I am disgusted that a new tragedy is here with me.

But with time and distance, I can look back on these events, and am able to see the good that came out of them.

LEARNING THE LESSONS FROM MISTAKES

If you make mistakes then undo them; learn from them. When I was fired from the North Carolina school, it took me 53 weeks to find another job. I took the time off to think and learn, and I refused to go back to another unhappy job. I looked at what was right for me, and then I analyzed why I had continued to work in jobs that did not fit.

I asked myself these questions: What did I want to achieve? How could I contribute to society and still have a job I was happy with?

"Adversity is the source of strength."

• Benjamin Franklin •

As I grew over the year, the vision of what I wanted to do became clearer. I deserved to be happy. So I looked for employment that supported my strengths and allowed for my limitations, and I found a vital job.

As I had overcome a violent marriage and survived, I could also overcome being fired from a job that was not right for me. No longer did I have to be a victim. I dealt with the pain and now I was going to move on with my life.

REFLECTIVE EXERCISE

- What causes you pain?
- Are you stuck in that pain?
- How can you move on with your life?
- What can make your life happier?

CHAPTER 6

Achieve Solutions

"Constant success shows us but one side of the world; adversity brings out the reverse of the picture."

• Colton •

Thriving Message Number 6

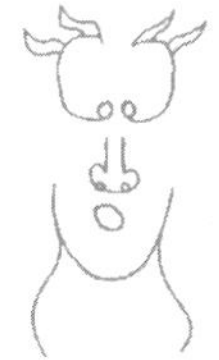

Break all your problems down to a workable size.

Years ago, I gave a speech at a very large corporation — and I bombed. It was the biggest bomb of my career. I got up in front of 161 people and I forgot what I was going to talk about. My mind went totally blank!

I stood in front of that audience and could not remember why I was there. When I finally said something, someone yelled out, "I can't hear you!" I fumbled around for some more words and my 45 minute keynote speech was 12 minutes long. The next day, I called the man who hired me to apologize. He asked if I was sick, because a large portion of the audience had asked him if I was sick. I said no, and he got off the phone in a hurry.

At first, I beat myself up. For five days and five sleepless nights I was a mess. I played it over and over in my head. What should I have done differently? By the fifth day, I was tired, looked terrible, and felt sick.

I picked up my pen and wrote down each mistake, giving birth to the Thriving Maps. (The instructions for this technique are found in chapter 17.) Then, I made a list of the ways I could prevent these mistakes from ever happening again. I learned from the mistakes of that terrible day and moved on.

There are still moments when I look back at that experience and want to die all over again, but then I think to myself, "Have I made those same mistakes since that day?" Every time, the answer is "No!"

"Whether you think you can or think you can't–you are right."
• Henry Ford •

To thrive you need to review what happened. You can't process and learn until you examine an event.

REFLECTIVE EXERCISE

- Refer to the list of problems you wrote in Chapter Three. Take each problem and seek solutions by creating a Thriving Map. (Instructions start on page 81.)

CHAPTER 7

Practice Humor

"Among those whom I like
or admire, I can find no
common denominator,
but among those whom I love,
I can: all of them make me laugh."

• W. H. Auden •

Thriving Message Number 7

Seek the freedom of humor.

There is an internationally known speaker who lives nearby and a few years ago I asked him if he would come and speak to a women's group to which I belonged. I was a bit nervous the day of his speech because I was going to introduce him.

A few days before the meeting, I went to a boutique and told the owner that when I get nervous, I sometimes perspire a bit more. She suggested going to a fabric shop and getting some perspiration pads to put in my clothes. She assured me that they worked for other people.

I guess I did not read the directions correctly. Before the speech, the speaker and I were talking and I glanced down toward my feet. I was shocked to see one of the pads lying on the floor.

He noticed it the same time as I did. What was I going to do? Very calmly I said, "Hey, you get the craziest garbage around here!" I then bent over and turned around, putting the pad in my pocket. The speaker thought I had put it in the waste basket. We continued talking and a few minutes later I excused myself and went to the ladies room. I took the other pad out so I wouldn't be embarrassed again.

Seeing the humor helps me get out of uncomfortable moments – especially my dyslexic moments, the moments when I'm thinking one thing and talking about another or I'm pointing left but I mean right.

"Many a man who could have been a success sleeps in a failure's grave today because he took life too seriously."

• Orison Swett Marden •

When I acknowledged I had dyslexia, I thought that was that, now I can go on with my life. But I was wrong. Dyslexia is with me every day and it is still an uphill battle.

So, what do I do when I make a crazy, dyslexic mistake? I laugh about myself – with myself and with others. I use it to my advantage. I might say something like "This dyslexic moment was brought to you by Margot Robinson!" And when I laugh, most people join in and laugh with me.

"Laughter is a gift from heaven."

• Orison Swett Marden •

Another example of this occurs when I begin training programs. I stand beside a flipchart and say, "I am a creative person. I know most of you know that. As a matter of fact, I have won an award for innovation. My most innovative area is spelling. So if you see any word that I've spelled that is not spelled the way you spell it, remember, I'm creative!" People always laugh and it gets me out of a potentially embarrassing moment.

What I learned is that if I don't laugh about something different I do, people begin to wonder about me. They might not follow my train of thought and then will judge me inappropriately.

My dyslexia will never go away. But I have the choice to use humor or not as I cope with it. Usually I choose to use the humor, which puts others at ease.

Humor is important not only when you are dealing with your problems, but in everyday life. The more you laugh, the better life is.

REFLECTIVE EXERCISE

- Think of experiences where humor could have eased you out of an embarrassing moment. Write these experiences down.
- Keep thinking about how you can use humor in your everyday life.

CHAPTER 8

Beyond Coping

"Nothing can bring you peace but yourself."

· Ralph Waldo Emerson ·

Thriving Message Number 8

Believe that everything is in your life for a reason.

I was so upset last summer. One week I didn't know I had diabetes, and the next week I did. Since I became aware of the problem, my life had not gone well. I was ill. I was angry. I cried a lot. I kept on asking, "Why now? Haven't I gone through enough pain to last a lifetime? What is going on here?"

I grabbed a piece of paper and just sat still. Then, I wrote these words, "Everything is working out the way it needs to be." I drew a heart around it and placed some color around the drawing. A few days later, I cut it out and put it in a frame. I put it on my desk so I could look at it every day.

A few months later, I sat down with a pad of paper and started a thriving map. (Technique begins on page 81.) I placed my life in a circle and then wrote all that was involved in my life — the good and the bad.

Even though I had just discovered that I had diabetes, I had much to be thankful for. I created a big picture of my life and it was good. I had succeeded again at acceptance, and I had realized that there was a reason for everything. It was not as bad as I thought it was.

Can I learn to thrive now that I have accepted my life as it is? Yes I can! Inner harmony and my new peaceful soul were staring me in the face. I became thankful for everything — the good and the bad, the total picture of my life.

"God helps them that help themselves."
• Benjamin Franklin •

REFLECTIVE EXERCISE

- Create a Thriving Map of your life. (See page 81 for directions.) Use the signs for positive (+) and negative (-) with each area you list.
- Look at the map. What is it telling you?
- Is your life more positive than you thought? Is it more negative?
- What can you do to change the negatives into positives?

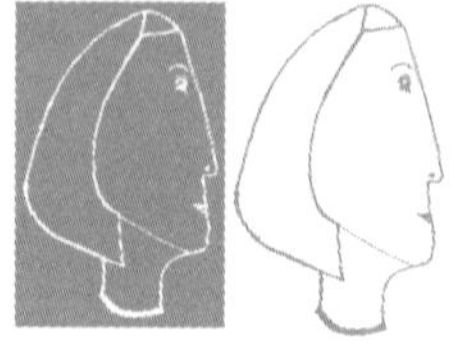

CHAPTER 9

Find the Real You

> "The pain of the mind is worse than the pain of the body."
>
> • Syrus •

Thriving Message Number 9

Free yourself from your self-imposed prison.

After graduating from a junior college, I went to live in Connecticut for a year before I returned to college to get my undergraduate degree. Being on my own and in my first apartment was so scary. I wasn't prepared for the real world, nor did I know who I was or where I was going. With almost no self-confidence, I was working for a bank and barely making it. I felt like a rubber band, ready to snap any minute.

One day a customer called the bank manager and told him about a "girl" who was very rude to her. He better straighten her out or she would take her business someplace else. He came over to me and explained what happened, and I burst into tears. All the bank customers were staring, and I heard someone say, "What is the matter with her?" I was quickly escorted into the lunch room and told to sit down and get a hold of myself.

Two weeks later I found out that a woman who was hired the same day I was got a raise and I didn't. As a matter of fact, I was the third worst teller in the history of the bank. Why should I get a raise?

As crazy as it seemed, I thought I deserved one. It didn't matter how poorly I was doing. That night I went home and got into a hot bath — with a knife in my hand. I didn't want to live any longer, but the knife wouldn't do anything. I couldn't kill myself. I called up my father the next day and told him I was having trouble. He suggested I take the day off and go to the hospital to see a counselor. My father gave me good advice. The counselor helped me see that I had created a world view that was not right - it was time for me to create another one.

"Often times the test of courage becomes to live, than to die."

· Alfieri ·

WHO WAS I?

For years I tried to discover who I wanted to be.

What were my gifts? Which way was I to go? I knew I wanted to stop being unhappy with my life, but what was the next step? At this point I realized that I, alone, had created the prison in which I lived. My family couldn't understand why there was so much turmoil in my life. They had always been loving and kind to me. How could my prison exist? But in my mind my prison did exist, and therefore, it was real.

"Conversation enriches the understanding, but solitude is the school of genius."

• Gibbon •

I began asking my friends and family what my strengths were. I began to see patterns in their answers. I took time to look at those patterns and to think. I paid more attention to my gifts — the ones that I was aware of and the ones my friends and family suggested I had.

As I began to be more aware of who I was, I continued to ask my friends: "Do you see me as someone who

______________________________?"

I filled in the blank, and I got the feedback I craved.

Instead of psychologically beating myself when I made mistakes, I asked: "Why do I continue to do ______________________________?", or, "Why can't I move from this stuck place to be more free?"

I paid attention to it all. I wrote about these issues in a journal, and I talked into a cassette player and recorded my deep, dark thoughts. It was an intense time.

"It has been my observation that people are just about as happy as they make up their minds to be."

• Abraham Lincoln •

The overwhelming answer that came to me was that if I did not get out of this pain soon, I would be overcome by it. Only then did I realize that I would have to free myself from the pain of my prison.

But there was one painful thought that kept coming back. It told me that I could not be truly happy unless I had someone with whom to share my life with. It said that I was no one without someone.

I looked for that someone at every party and every event. I looked everywhere to find that someone, but I kept finding the wrong one.

Ultimately, I learned to take charge of my life. Why did I need to continue to seek happiness from someone else, when I could create that happiness from within? Then I realized I could be — and was — truly happy without a man. I could create my own happiness.

Two weeks later, I met my second husband.

"Our first and last love is – self love."

• Bovee •

He was ready to settle down, and told me so on our first date. I said "NO WAY! I just found out that I can be happy being me and living alone. You can't take my new freedom away from me." One year later we were married.

The self-discovery process was finding myself and learning what I wanted out of life. I got in touch with my gifts and lived them. I learned from my mistakes and went on. I asked people for feedback so that I could see in the mirror what was being projected. I looked at the pain and asked if it needed to be in my life. Then I asked how I could defuse the pain and go on. I sought to find the real me.

REFLECTIVE EXERCISE

- Look for feedback from others. Ask friends, family and business associates to list your strengths and limitations.
- Thank them, even if the information is uncomfortable to receive. It is also uncomfortable to give.
- Then look at this feedback. How can it help you break out of whatever self-imposed prison you're in?
- Seek to find the real you.

CHAPTER 10

Just Be

"Human improvement is from within outward."

• Froude •

Thriving Message Number 10

Be alone, rest, and think.

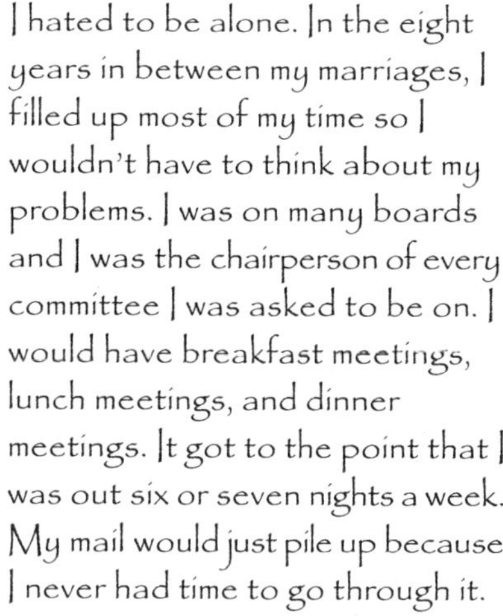

I hated to be alone. In the eight years in between my marriages, I filled up most of my time so I wouldn't have to think about my problems. I was on many boards and I was the chairperson of every committee I was asked to be on. I would have breakfast meetings, lunch meetings, and dinner meetings. It got to the point that I was out six or seven nights a week. My mail would just pile up because I never had time to go through it.

My second husband couldn't understand why I was so busy. Every weekend I had an agenda, so we would have every minute packed.

One of the best things my husband taught me was to "just be". He fought me long and hard about the weekends. "Please no agendas," he would say. "How can you get anything done if you don't have an agenda?", I asked. As the years passed, I learned the value of "just being" — to listen to the sounds, to be in the moment, and to reflect back on what was and then reflect on what is to be.

"Time was made for slaves."
• John B. Buckston •

AS THE WORLD GOES BY

The world seems to spin faster and faster every day. What was fast three or four years ago is slow today. It seems that all we can do is just hang on and try to survive.

We go through the motions of life, but we become tired. We have problems that are overwhelming, and at times we seem to just exist. But life is more than just existing. There is more meaning to life than just keeping your head above water.

We need to live a more balanced life — a balance between activity and rest. Most of us are good about activity; it is rest that we need to work on.

When I first came across this concept, I thought rest meant just "hanging out" and being alone, which really did not appeal to me. Again, I hated to be alone. In order to avoid it, I just didn't spend any time by myself.

Now I take time "to be". Sometimes my thoughts are

painful, but if I do not take time to just be, I won't be aware of what is going on inside me.

Not only does taking time just "to be" help me get in touch with my emotions, it also helps me create strategies for making my life more meaningful. Taking time to reflect is essential. Without it, I would live with a cluttered mind, which is not conducive to a peaceful soul.

"All that we are is the result of what we have thought; it is founded on our thoughts; it is made up of our thoughts."

• Buddhist Proverb •

REFLECTIVE EXERCISE

- Look at all areas of your life. What can you do to create more time to rest and be alone?
- Write down any ideas that come to mind.

CHAPTER 11

Live in the Moment

"What good thing have I done this day? The setting sun will carry with it a portion of my life."

• Hindi Proverb •

Thriving Message Number 11

Live in this very moment.

I was stationed in Hawaii during my Army days. One night, my former husband and I had a terrible fight. The next day I decided to take the day off from work and be with my German shepherd. We went to the North Shore on Oahu to have some fun in the sun.

It was on this special day that I had a "just be in the moment" experience. The South Pacific was green, aqua, and blue all together. The gentle Kona breeze blew and the ocean was very calm. My dog Kilo (which means Watchful in Hawaiian) and I decided to swim. We swam parallel to the ocean shore and then turned around and swam back. He was right next to me, swimming along as my silent companion. The moment was perfect — I felt intensely alive.

I realized the natural order of the universe was all around me. I could hear the birds singing, waves splashing, and children yelling with glee. I realized I could be silent and listen.

When we came back to the beach, I sat down and wrote this poem.

"Life" I say
"Life?" he said
"Yes life" I say
"Whose life?" he said
"My life" I say
"Your life?" he said
"My life is mighty fine!" I say
"Mighty fine?"
"A fire in my heart" I say
"Fire?" he said
"Tingles" I say
"Tingles?"
"Rushes" I say
"And?"
"Goodness forever!" I say
"Goodness!"
"Charisma always" I say
"Always!"
"Love everlasting!" I say
"Lasting!"
"Forever and ever" I say
"And ditto for that!"
"Hey it's great to be alive" I say

"Ah yes!"

No matter how hard life gets, that poem, especially the two lines, "My life is mighty fine!" and "Ah Yes!" gets me through.

"All Nature wears one universal grin."

• Henry Fielding •

" No longer forward nor behind I look in hope or fear; but grateful, take the good I find the best of now and here."

• John Greenleaf Whittier •

Accepting diabetes brought back how important it is to live in the moment. When I became overwhelmed with sadness over having this illness, I thought about living right now, not tomorrow, not yesterday but right now. I got in touch with my five senses – sound, smell, taste, touch, and vision. And in that moment I lived.

THE MONK

My favorite story of living in the moment is about a Buddhist Monk who fell off a cliff. A branch snagged his jacket and kept him suspended. Next to the branch was a patch of wild strawberries. The Monk took delight in tasting those fine, wild strawberries. He marvelled at how excited he was to find such an unusual patch. The branch snapped and he fell to his death. Though facing death, this Buddhist Monk lived truly in the moment.

When I live in the moment, life has more meaning. Yesterday was yesterday – tomorrow is tomorrow, but today is the only moment in my life that I can really live.

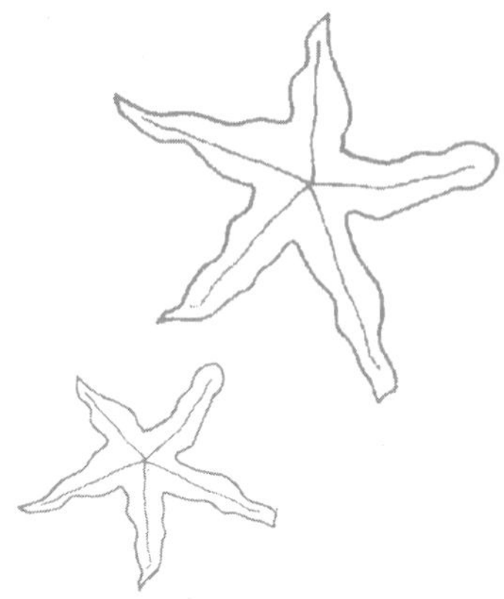

" All art, all education, can be merely a supplement to nature."

• Aristotle •

NATURE

Being alone, within the natural order of the world, is one of the most clearing experiences we can have. No matter what kind of mood I am experiencing, if I walk within that natural world, my mood becomes softer and I become more peaceful. I get in touch with my thoughts when I am in the world of nature and I examine what is happening in my world. By examining my life, I have the opportunity to look at myself and seek solutions. Without examination, the ruts remain deep and the dark clouds continue to rain.

The more I am in nature, the more answers come to me. Nature affects – activates – my subconscious. It speeds up the healing process. When I can just be in the moment with nature, I am surrounded with inspiration.

I took a walk a few weeks ago, when for some reason a dark cloud was hanging over my head. Suddenly, I heard something in the bushes, and there in front of me was a herd of deer. They took

off and ran up a hill to a meadow. I was excited to be in that moment — oh yes, that moment. The rest of the walk was just that — living in the moment.

I know it is difficult to live in the moment all the time. But the more I can, the more alive I am. I know this will be true for you, too.

REFLECTIVE EXERCISE

- Today, spend one hour living in the moment. Be aware of all of your senses — sounds, smells, tastes, touch, and vision.
- When something from the past or future comes to mind, come back to the moment and try not to think about other things on your mind.
- When the hour is up, ask yourself: What was it like? How did I feel?
- It takes practice to live in the moment. At first it will be hard, but with practice you will get many rewards. What are they?
- Write down what you learned about living in the moment.

CHAPTER 12

The Positive Umbrella

"I think, therefore I am."

· Descartes ·

Thriving Message Number 12

Surround yourself with positive energy.

A few years back, a friend and I got so disgusted with all the negativity around us, that we decided to create a business called Positives, Inc. We would make a series of television shows that talked about the positives in people's lives, thoughts, and emotions.

Well, it was only a dream and it died. But from that moment on, I realized that being around positive energy nurtured my soul. If I was with negative people, I became negative. But if I was with positive people, I felt more charged, more alive, and excited about life.

I think every moment has an emotional overtone to it. I call it an "emotional umbrella". If I want happiness in my life, I create a positive umbrella.

I know that sometimes it is difficult to have a positive umbrella. Sometimes the "stuff" gets too heavy and all around you it is just raining negatives. But the faster you can grab onto a positive thought or be with a positive person, the better your day will be and the more enjoyable you are to be around.

"Keep your face to the sunshine and you cannot see the shadows."

• Helen Keller •

Negative energy is very draining; positive energy is very uplifting. I seek a positive overtone in everything I do — most of the time I win.

If I find myself in a negative mood, or with a negative person, I can change. If it is a thought, the first step is to visualize that positive umbrella around me. I take some deep breaths and visualize the negative leaving with every exhale.

If I am with a negative person, I bow out of the conversation as soon as I can and think of that positive umbrella around me. I seek people who are positive. The more my emotions are in the positive range, the more gratification I will experience in my life.

REFLECTIVE EXERCISE

- What steps do you need to take to create more positives in your life?
- Can you visualize a positive umbrella?
- Write down those situations in which you can change negative energy into positive energy.

CHAPTER 13

Let Your Spirit Sing

"Imagination is more important than knowledge."

- Albert Einstein -

Thriving Message Number 13

Allow your spirit's song to be sung.

The month before I realized I had diabetes, I had a lot of creative dreams. During my waking hours I had a strong desire to do something creative, but I did not have the energy to do it. Months before, my husband and I were building a house in rural North Carolina. I had put so much energy into the house that I had cut myself off from a lot — mostly my spirit. I pondered about the best creative activity I could come up with that would not take a lot of energy.

I picked up a whittling knife and headed down toward the stream at the back of our property. I found a piece of wood and carved a figure I called the "Goddess of Creativity" and placed her on the sandbank.

The ceremony had begun. I was asking to receive my creativity back again. The dark cloud lifted. The thoughts of fear and despair were not as prevalent now. My spirit's song began to sing once again.

"Take a music bath once or twice a week for a few seasons, and you will find that it is to the soul what the water bath is to the body."

• Oliver Wendell Holmes •

GETTING OUT OF THE BOX

One night shortly after my Goddess of Creativity – ceremony, I was standing outside our new house, looking inside. I thought about how different it looked to me. I had always thought of the house from the perspective of standing inside and looking out into the woods.

Then it hit me. My life was stuck because I was only looking at it from one way – the inside out. When I looked inside my life, from outside in, I saw a different potential. The creative ideas and thoughts opened up. I began to be free from a stuck place.

Creativity unlocks doors that have been bolted shut. I celebrate me. I decorate my office with notes of my spirit's song. I dress in casual attire that states who I am. I pick up colored pens and draw without a purpose. I dance around my house with my favorite music. I let my spirit sing. The more I open myself up to creativity, the more I will be the individual I am meant to be.

Creativity helps the peaceful process prosper. It makes life more delightful. Rich lives flow from creative spirits. The more creatively I approach my life, the richer my life will be. Creativity unlocks the door to my soul. Without creativity, without living outside the box, the less likely I am to find new solutions to my problems.

" The discovery of what is true and the practice of that which is good are the two most important objects of philosophy."

• Voltaire •

REFLECTIVE EXERCISE

- Make a list for each of the following questions:
- How has your life been stuck?
- How can you let your spirit's song be sung?
- Can you think of a time when you were in touch with your spirit?
- What did it feel like?
- How can you regain that feeling?

CHAPTER 14

It's Your Life – Celebrate

"A true friend is one soul in two bodies."

• Aristotle •

Thriving Message Number 14

Take time to celebrate the little things in life.

I called my grandmother KK. She taught me about unconditional love.

When I was four years old, my sister received a record album for Christmas. For some reason, I did not like the record. I picked it up and broke it in half. My father, my mom, and my sister were very upset with me. They yelled at me, and rightfully so.

Then KK talked to me. She didn't yell. (As a matter of fact, I never recall her yelling at me while I was growing up.) "Why did you break that record?" she asked. I told her I didn't like it. Then she asked me, "How do you think your sister is feeling right now?" I hadn't thought about that. She told me, "Even though you should not have broken the record, I still love you!"

No matter what I did, KK was always in my corner. She loved me — unconditionally. I felt safer with her than with anyone else.

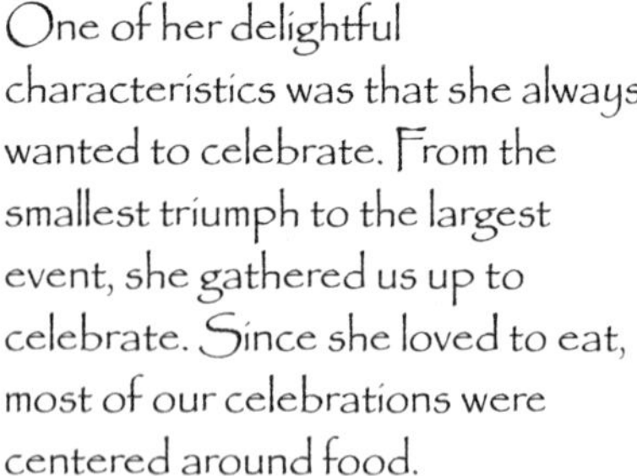

One of her delightful characteristics was that she always wanted to celebrate. From the smallest triumph to the largest event, she gathered us up to celebrate. Since she loved to eat, most of our celebrations were centered around food.

Her favorite place to take me for an everyday celebration was a little hamburger shack in Schenectady, New York. We would order the "Blue Plate Special" and I always felt like a queen for the day when I ate it with her. We certainly were lucky to be able to celebrate together and have a "Blue Plate Special". Life could not get any better than this!

" People seldom improve when they have no other model but themselves to copy after."

• Goldsmith •

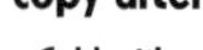

As a child, it was a real treat to go and spend the night at KK's. She would celebrate our time together by making a doll out of rubber bands and a dish rag. Every doll was different and I got to sleep with each one.

After she made me the doll, she would tell me that she was the

"Children have more need of models than of critics."
• Joubert •

strongest grandmother in the world. Of course a small child would believe this silly statement. Then she asked me if I wanted to see her muscle. With much glee I would say yes. I sat up in bed, my eyes big. KK would make a strange noise and then a big muscle would pop up!

It took me years to understand how she got that muscle. You see she had a lot of extra skin on her arm. She would push the skin up and it would appear to be a huge muscle.

I would always laugh and tell everyone my grandmother was probably the strongest grandmother in the world. I really believed it. She loved having me tell others about her strength.

Now KK was not known for her cooking. But every time I had dinner at her apartment, we would have my favorite meal, lamb chops. I thought I had died and gone to heaven because I had my favorite meal with my favorite person!

When I remember her, I always think of our celebrations. These times will always ride with me in my heart, and I can still hear her say, "Let's celebrate!" Just before she died, she became senile. But we would sing the suffragette songs that she taught me, and we would laugh together as much as we could. One day when I went to see her, she was thinking very clearly. "You know Margot", she said. "you and I have always been very close. We have had a certain bond between us." I assured her that she was right. I saw her only twice more.

"It's love, it's love that makes the world go round."

• French Song •

KK died at the age of 93. My journal entry for that day was, "My KK died this morning. I miss her already....She taught me how to love ....and celebrate."

REFLECTIVE EXERCISE

- What are ways that you can start celebrating your life?
- Make a list and starting today, incorporate them in your life.

CHAPTER 15

Extra Strength

"Faith is the force of life."

• Tolstoy •

Thriving Message Number 15

Call on a higher power for extra strength.

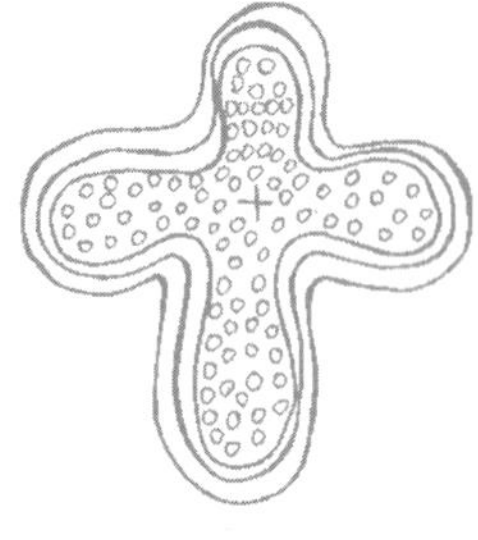

I remember it as if it happened yesterday. After I was fired from my job at the state school in North Carolina, I sat in silence. Then I cried, I screamed, and I prayed. I felt that I could not go on any more. But I felt a calm that I had never felt before - or since. It was a calm that told me everything would be all right.

It was then that my spiritual journey began.

My spiritual journey has been full of wise spirits or angels watching over me. These entities care about me and I feel their energy around me. They bring me the peace and strength I need.

I believe it is important during hard times to call on a higher power. You might call this power God, Jesus, Buddha, or whatever, but I call it my higher power. If I didn't have the strength of my higher power during exceptionally hard times, it would be almost impossible for me to pull through.

"A man does not live a hundred years, yet he worries enough for a thousand."

• Chinese Proverb •

CLEANSING THE SOUL

In the beginning of my diabetes journey, when I was ill from high blood sugar, I had a hard time working. When you are self-employed, you are responsible for doing everything. I could not even get on the phone to market my business. Most of the time I would lay on the couch. Then I began to realize that money was not coming in. We had just finished building our house. Where was the money going to come from to pay our bills? Two years before, my husband had started his business and it had yet to make a profit.

I became ill from worry. I was not sleeping well and I had an upset stomach from not knowing how we were going to make it.

It was during this time that I discovered the hot air balloon. I realized that I needed to have a clear heart and mind from this worry. To clear myself from this torment, I imagined this situation going into a hot air balloon and floating away.

“ **The person who has a firm trust in the Supreme Being is powerful in his power, wise by his wisdom, happy by his happiness.”**

- William Adams -

You see, I am not strong enough to handle everything. If the problem is too big, I send it off to my higher power, who takes care of the problem for me.

Thriving means cleansing the soul, and if the problem stays, my soul remains dark. In order to live, I need a clear soul. It doesn't mean that the situation is gone forever — it means that I have sent the situation out in the hot air balloon.

After putting my work and money issues out to pasture, I could live a full life without worry, making it easier for me to concentrate on getting my health back. It was amazing that things worked out just the way they needed to. I took time off because of my illness, and when I was ready to go back to work, opportunities began to open up for me.

That hot air balloon is very handy to have around. Now I do not have so much weight on my shoulders. I am free to live in the moment. I am free to be at peace.

REFLECTIVE EXERCISE

- Take time to reflect on your higher self. How do you get extra strength from it?
- Visualize yourself giving a problem to your higher self and watch it float away as if it were in the hot air balloon. Keep that vision in your head until it is time to call it back from the air.

" We walk by faith, not by sight."

• II Corinthians V:7 •

CHAPTER 16

Your Journey

"When we look into the long avenue of the future, and see the good there is for each one of us to do, we realize, after all, what a beautiful thing it is to work, and to live and to be happy."

• Robert Louis Stevenson •

Thriving Message Number 16

Become the expert of your journey.

I do not have all the answers. I am not an expert in anything except my own journey. I do know that once I learned to be at peace, my world thrived. I have faith that if you want to change, you will.

Only you have the power to create the life you want and deserve. I know that some problems seem overwhelming and look as if they will never go away. But if you learn to cope with them, your life will flourish.

In order to clean up that heavy cloud around you, I created this review list to help you get to the garden sooner. It is when your are in the garden that you will blossom.

1. You are responsible for your own thoughts and actions.
2. Feel the pain; do not run away from it.
3. Free yourself from your self-imposed prison.
4. Surround yourself with positive energy.
5. Break the problem up into small workable solutions by creating "Thriving Maps."
6. Send the problem off to your higher power. If the problem comes back, send it out again until it stops haunting you.
7. Be open and listen for answers within.
8. Live in the moment.
9. Celebrate your life.

"Patience–in time the grass becomes milk"

• Chinese Proverb •

CHAPTER 17

Developing Thriving Skills

> **"The great end of life is not knowledge but action."**
>
> • Thomas Henry Huxley •

Thriving Message Number 17

You hold all the answers within — just listen.

In order for you to get started on your healing journey, I have created some thriving skills. They have helped me and others through our hard times. Use these skills along with the reflective exercises at the end of each chapter. I recommend that you develop what feels right to you and skip over parts with which you don't connect. I want you to create the healing experiences that are right for you.

STRESS

By seeking solutions, you can go beyond the problem. But sometimes there is a big roadblock that makes seeking solutions impossible. That roadblock is stress. Stress muddies the waters to clear solutions. When your mind is anxious, your solutions are lost.

In today's world, it's hard not to have stress. But we need to "de-stress" before we create Thriving Maps.

Below are some ideas to help you "de-stress" before you begin your self discovery.

1. Sit in a quiet place. If the space is noisy, tune out the noise around you by playing soothing music.

2. Close your eyes.

3. Take a deep belly breath. (Put your hand on your stomach and take a deep breath. When you feel your belly go up from the breath, then you are belly breathing.) Three or four good belly breaths should create more calmness around you. Now open your eyes.

Now you are ready to create a Thriving Map.

THRIVING MAPS

When you get into your car to go to an unfamiliar place, you need to look at a map in order to get there. You do not just get in the car and go. If you do, there's a good chance you'll get lost. Maps give you guidelines for where you are going.

In order to have the best experience with creating a Thriving Map follow these steps:

1. Buy a notebook with plain, unlined paper.
2. Buy colored pens. (The pens help the creative process, but you can get along with just a pencil or pen.) Use a different color pen for each solution.
3. Write any issue that you are having problems with in the center and then circle it.
4. Some solutions might have three or four points. Write them all down.
5. Do not judge any idea or solution that comes to mind. One idea might stimulate another idea. Write down everything.
6. Attach every solution to the problem with a spoke.
7. Each Thriving Map addresses one problem. Keep it simple. It will become clearer and easier to understand the problem by using a simple approach.

THRIVING MAPS: AN EXAMPLE

By writing in a free association form, solutions or ideas will appear, which gives you the opportunity to see the big picture more clearly. Ideas that you really hadn't noticed will be the most obvious.

If you would like to go into more detail, write a sentence or two about each thought on another piece of paper. This detail will help you get in touch with your emotions. Once the emotions are exposed, solutions can take place faster.

LISTENING TO YOUR SUBCONSCIOUS

You may live in a city where it is hard to be around nature. Even a trip to the local park or the roof top might be difficult. What can you do to help you listen to your subconscious?

Here is a process I developed for being in the moment and tapping into the subconscious.

Step One: Get a pad of paper and a pen.

Step Two: Sit in a quiet place.

Step Three: Create questions that need answers and write them down. Close your eyes and take 2-3 deep belly breaths. Then open your eyes.

Step Four: Read the first question and then close your eyes and just listen. If something comes to mind, write it down. Do not question the response — just write what comes to mind. Go to the next question and repeat the process. Do not ask more than four questions at each session.

Step Five: Review the responses and think about the messages you received. Two or three times during that day, come back to what you wrote. Write down any conclusions you draw from the material you received.

Keep a journal of the questions and answers. It's a good idea to date every response so that when you go back to read them, you're not wondering, "When did I write this?"

I say a prayer before I start. I believe there is negative energy out there. Praying helps seek positive energy and will bring the right answers.

Once this technique is perfected, you will be able to listen to your intuitive or subconscious mind more easily. For over twelve years I have gained much information by using this technique.

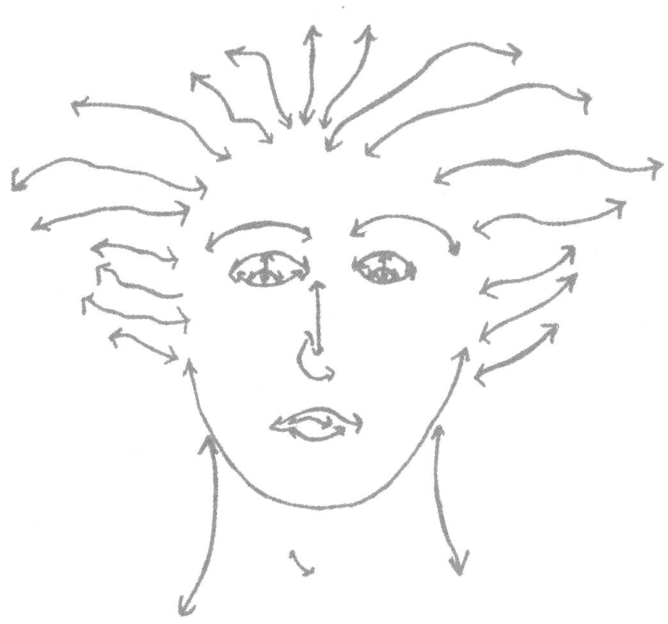

CHAPTER 18

Conclusion

"The two words, 'peace' and 'tranquility' are worth a thousand pieces of gold."

• Chinese Proverb •

Be aware of the voice inside, for it will tell you your truth. Your life should be a process of finding the right truth for you. Ralph Waldo Emerson once wrote, "To believe your own thought, to believe that what is true for you in your private heart is true for all men, — that is genius."

Take time from your busy life to find your genius. When you find your true inner self, life has more meaning — more joy.

Your inner pain is there for a reason. Discover what the pain means, and then release it. Learn from it and then let go of it. You do not need to carry a painful banner the rest of your life.

Life is like a garden and though even in the garden there are thorns, there is beauty, too. Seek the beauty in each and every thing that comes across your path of life, knowing that

"**Reader farewell, all happiness attend thee; may each New Year, better and richer find thee.**"

• Benjamin Franklin •

some things will be more challenging than others. Find the principles that you can live by. Stand up for them; make them known to others. Remember that if you are like everyone else, the world loses out on not knowing the beauty of the true you and that is a real loss.

Take the time to awaken your soul. Become aware of the world around you, and then do everything in your power to be at peace. You deserve it. Life has been given to you by the divine architect — all you have to do is find your purpose.

The exercises in this book will help you with your process. Take the time to do each exercise. Create a notebook that will help you start the journey of awakening your soul.

As I close, I wish you peace, balance, love, joy, health, and wealth. May you find your peaceful soul within.

Other books by
MARGOT ROBINSON

EGOS & EGGSHELLS:
Managing For Success
In Today's Workplace

For more information about workshops or to get in touch with Margot Robinson, write: P.O. Box 21585, Greensboro, NC 27420-1585.

Design: Peter Hollingsworth & Associates
Cover Photo: Willa Stein Back Cover: David Amundson